TRINITY GESE GRADE 10
CONVERSATION PHASE

A GUIDE FOR STUDENTS AND TEACHERS

PETER ASHBY

For all my students, past and present, who have inspired me to write this book.

CONTENTS

INTRODUCTION

With the demand for higher-level English language qualifications for the purposes of accessing employment and educational programmes becoming ever greater, the Trinity GESE (Graded Skills In Spoken English) examinations are a popular choice. This examination offers the candidate the opportunity to gain an internationally recognised qualification in spoken English without the need to pass a reading, writing and grammar component. It is therefore sometimes seen as a more convenient and time-friendly option. However, both students and teachers frequently encounter problems when preparing for these examinations due to the limited amount of practice material available from publishers as well as on the internet.

Based on my considerable experience as a teacher of English as a second language and drawing on the experiences and comments of my students, I have produced this resource book as a companion volume to **Trinity GESE 10 Listening Phase** and **Trinity GESE 10 Interactive Phase**, which I hope will prove useful both in the classroom and for those who wish to practice at home. It contains many useful tips, examples and detailed advice aimed at improving performance in the GESE 10 conversation phase, along with 120 conversation task prompts to practice in class, at home or during language exchanges.

Importantly, it also includes a section which explains in detail the essential language functions required at Level 10, as well as a review of the language functions for Level 9. Because the advice given is based directly on the experiences, comments and feedback of my Trinity GESE and ISE students, it therefore directly reflects the issues which they themselves have identified.

USEFUL INFORMATION

WHO IS THIS BOOK FOR?

This book is primarily aimed at GESE 10 (Common European Framework of Reference C1) students and teachers, but it may also be useful for those preparing to take the GESE Grades 11 and 12 and ISE III (Integrated Skills in English) speaking examinations.

The advice regarding functional language and the practice prompts will also be of use to any advanced student of English when preparing to take a recognised examination or looking to improve their general language skills.

WHICH EXAM IS THE RIGHT ONE FOR ME?

New English examinations are being introduced all the time, and choosing the right one for yourself can sometimes be a very confusing decision. The Trinity exams - GESE and ISE (Integrated Skills in English) are internationally recognised and respected and are among the most widely accepted English language qualifications.

Being able to communicate effectively in English in fields as diverse as business, education, research, diplomacy, translation and the arts is becoming increasingly important in the age of globalisation, and GESE is particularly suitable if you need to express this ability. It is one of the few examinations that focuses specifically on verbal English skills with a short listening component: furthermore, the tasks are designed to assess language skills in the manner that they are used in a wide range of everyday contexts.

If you require an English qualification in order to apply to a university or other educational establishment, when preparing a job application for a specific employer or for any other official purpose, **ALWAYS** check with them which examinations they do and do not accept. In addition to this, some countries do not recognise certain qualifications (for example, this may be an issue in the United States of America as their own TOEFL English examination is usually accepted over UK-based qualifications) so it is vital to find this out beforehand so as not to waste your time and money and to avoid disappointment.

WHEN WILL I BE READY TO TAKE THE EXAM?

This is one of the most important pieces of advice that I can give you. In my experience, most students who fail English examinations do so because they are not ready. There are a number of reasons for this.

The first is that they have unrealistic expectations or are too confident in their language abilities. The next is not understanding what they are expected to do in the exam - this might be due to a lack of preparation or having been given poor guidance by a teacher who also does not understand the exam very well.

Another issue is that language academies sometimes give their students guarantees that they will pass the examination within a relatively short period of time. Courses are offered that are sometimes too short to fulfil all of the student's needs. What is more, if you are part of a large group, it may not be possible to receive the individual attention that is so important when preparing for the GESE 10 examination.

Finally, students are frequently under enormous pressure to obtain a language certificate for study or employment purposes within a very short period of time. Leaving the English certificate until the last moment, however, is rarely a successful strategy.

The truth is that there is no "quick fix" to passing an examination in spoken English. We are all individuals and while one person might achieve the required level relatively quickly, for others this may be a long process. My advice is therefore to **always seek the advice of an experienced English teacher** before registering for an exam. The teacher will thoroughly evaluate your particular strengths and weaknesses and advise you when you are sufficiently prepared. Failure to do this can risk losing a large amount of money due to wasted examination fees and having to start all over again.

HOW TO USE THIS BOOK

This book can be used either as part of a structured class or for home use. If you are using it at home, you may want to ask a native English speaker or another high-level English user to practice with you.

DISCLAIMER

The author wishes to emphasise that this book is an unofficial study guide and is in no way connected with, or endorsed by, any examining body, academy or other institution. The material and advice it contains is based entirely on my own experience as an accomplished English teacher and on the invaluable feedback received from my students over the years.

GETTING STARTED

Although students sometimes choose to prepare for the GESE Level 10 examination because they think that it is an easier alternative to other popular English examinations that evaluate the four skills of reading, writing, speaking and listening, this is a serious mistake! After all, GESE 10 tests your ability to understand and communicate with spoken English at C1 level, and this requires an advanced understanding of all aspects of the language.

In my experience, even some fluent speakers who do not have much difficulty in directing and maintaining a conversation can have problems at this level when they need to demonstrate their abilities under examination conditions and use a set of skills which are specified by the examination board.

First of all, let's take a look at what you actually have to do in the GESE 10 conversation phase. This is the final part of the exam and it lasts for up to **six minutes**. There are two lists of subject areas - **List A** and **List B** - each one containing six possible subjects. The candidate only needs to prepare one of these lists and should be ready to discuss any two subjects selected by the examiner from the chosen list.

List A	List B
Roles in the family	International events
Communication	Equal opportunities
The school curriculum	Social issues
Youth behaviour	The future of the planet
Use of the internet	Scientific developments
Designer goods	Stress management

The examiner will start the task by choosing one subject area from the chosen list and will introduce a question or statement about this subject by saying: "Let's talk about…"

The candidate and the examiner then exchange opinions, information and ideas about the subject for approximately three minutes. Then, the examiner changes the subject for discussion by saying: "Thank you. Now let's talk about..." After another three minutes, the examiner brings the conversation to an end.

During this task, you need to **share the responsibility** with the examiner for keeping the conversation going. Please remember that you are engaged in a **dialogue**, and a dialogue is a two-way process. Do not exclusively rely on the examiner to guide the conversation. The examiner needs to hear you using a range of language skills (we will be looking at these in detail later on) which will demonstrate your ability to maintain a natural and confident English conversation.

You need to do more than this, however. It is not enough simply to make comments about what the examiner has said to you, or even to agree, disagree and challenge the examiner's statements. You also need to **add new comments** in order to influence the direction of the conversation. In others words, **you** are in control of the conversation.

This is a C1 level speaking examination and you also need to demonstrate that you can use a wide range of expressions and vocabulary without having to think too much about what you are going to say. There are methods you can use to give yourself a few moments to think about what you are going to say but if you hesitate for too long, the examiner will not help you.

TIMING

Although the conversation phase lasts for up to six minutes, this means that you will only be talking about each subject for a maximum of **three minutes**.

Look at the beginning of <u>Conversation 1</u>, which is from List B (scientific developments):

Speaker A: To be honest, I think that there are a few scientific developments that should never have been discovered or invented. Don't you agree with me?

Speaker B: Yes, absolutely. One of them has to be atomic energy. I mean, atomic power led to the creation of the atom bomb and personally I don't think that nuclear weapons are a deterrent. They just make the world a more dangerous place to live in and they increase the likelihood of a nuclear war in the future. And another thing is that the risk of an accident at a nuclear power station is just too great.

Speaker A: Uh… I -

Speaker B: Look at what happens if something goes wrong? What about Chernobyl and Fukushima? These were really terrible accidents and people were killed in them. Not only that, the surrounding land is going to be poisoned for hundreds of years. I personally think that we need to be closing down all the nuclear power plants and focusing on clean, green energy - solar power, wind turbines, things like that. These don't damage the natural world and what's more, the sun and the wind will never run out.

Speaker B: Well, can I just say - ?

Speaker B: And another thing … (etcetera)

Speaker B made a number of fundamental mistakes which will affect the timing of this interaction. His comments were far too long and were in the form of a **monologue.** It is clear that if this were an examination task and Speaker A continued in this manner, Speaker B would have no opportunity to contribute and the three minutes would soon be over.

It is important for the candidate and the examiner to work together in order to reach a conclusion. Remember that you only have three minutes to do this. If you use all of this time to express your opinions, there will be no time left in which to resolve the dialogue and certainly no time to demonstrate the language functions required for this level.

We will be returning to this conversation later on.

RELEVANCE

Conversation 1 is an example of a prompt taken from List B: Scientific developments. Although Speaker B (the candidate) starts by expressing agreement with Speaker A (the examiner), towards the end of this extract they **deviate** from the original statement by talking about green energy sources, a field of scientific development that they clearly believe to be positive.

Although the candidate needs to direct the conversation, it is very important not to change the subject. In Conversation 1, it might seem that alternative energy such as solar power is linked with the general idea of scientific developments but the speaker has ignored the original statement which is related to those that should (in the speaker's opinion) never have been invented and discovered. Remember - you do not have time to deviate from the subject in three minutes so keep your contributions relevant.

Now look at Conversation 2:

Speaker 1: *I really think that the behaviour of young people today leaves a lot to be desired.*

Speaker 2: *Oh, you don't really think so, do you? Well, I'm not sure I agree with you but why don't you give me an example?*

Speaker 1: *For a start, you see a lot of teenagers out on the streets at night, just hanging around and getting into trouble.*

Speaker 2: *How do you know they're getting into trouble? Maybe they don't have anywhere else to go. There should be more youth clubs and sports facilities for them - things like that. Then they wouldn't have to hang around outside getting bored, would they?*

Speaker 1: *I guess you have a point there. Perhaps local councils should be doing more to keep them occupied. But even if they did, I still think that* *most teenagers are more interested in social networking than doing something constructive.*

Speaker 2: *Sorry to disagree with you, but I think that's a generalisation. In my town the young people have actually formed a community support group. They go round visiting old people, doing their shopping for them, all kinds of things like that… (etcetera)*

In this conversation on the subject of youth behaviour (List A), Speaker B makes her disagreement with the original statement clear but asks Speaker A to justify his point of view. She then responds by challenging Speaker A's reply and once again gives Speaker A the opportunity to defend his point of view. This is a balanced discussion and, importantly, Speaker B ensures that her comments are relevant to the original statement.

ACTIVE LISTENING

Conversation 3:

Speaker 1: *One of the biggest social problems in this country is the lack of affordable housing for young people.*

Speaker 2: *I think that young people don't have enough employment opportunities. Something needs to be done about it.*

Speaker 1: *Er… yes, I totally agree with you. But getting back to housing -*

Speaker 2: *I mean, it's not surprising that so many graduates have to go abroad to find work.*

In this short extract from a conversation about social issues (List B), Speaker 2 is not being a good listener. He has not made any comment about what Speaker 1 has said in relation to housing problems - the only information he has used from the original statement is "young people". This could mean that he did not understand what Speaker 1 was saying, but it could also be evidence that he was not focusing on the detailed information contained in her statement.

It is sometimes said that nowadays we are losing our ability to listen. Information in the media is frequently presented to us in the form of brief "soundbytes" - short statements - and we frequently do not take the time to concentrate on what others are saying to us. Active listening is a skill that you must develop, however, if you are to succeed in the GESE 10 examination. This does not simply mean that you have to listen without responding. It involves giving your complete attention to what is being said, demonstrating that you are listening, and responding in an appropriate manner.

If understanding spoken English is difficult for you, it is vital that you develop your listening skills. However, you must always **listen for a**

reason. Although watching series and documentaries in their original version format and listening to the English lyrics of songs might be useful for developing your general listening ability, in my opinion this is not enough to prepare you for the very specific tasks you need to do in the GESE 10 examination.

Fortunately, there are a number of useful exercises that you can do either at home or in the classroom that will assist you in building your focus. One of these involves listening to a short recording that has a complete written transcript. There are many excellent free resources online that you can use and one of my favourites is TED Talks. This is an incredible online resource consisting of thousands of short talks about almost every subject that you can think of, from science, society and sport to health, environmental issues and the arts. Each talk has a full transcript with a moving cursor that indicates exactly at what point you are:

www.ted.com/talks

The following exercise is very useful for practicing listening and comprehension and can also be used to prepare for the GESE 10 listening and interactive phases (see my other books in this series). Choose a **short** talk (four or five minutes is sufficient) and listen to it carefully without reading the transcript. As you listen, take some notes and try to identify the **main** ideas in the talk. If you need to listen twice, this is fine.

When you have done this, take a few minutes to use your notes in order to write a **brief** summary of what you have heard. Do not write more than three or four sentences. Once you have done this, listen again but this time, read the transcript at the same time. Check to see if you managed to summarise the main ideas of the recording.

Remember that you might have to spend a lot of time developing your listening skills. Attending a class is generally not sufficient. You need to make time in order to focus exclusively on practice. And remember - **always listen for a purpose.**

ASKING QUESTIONS

Conversation 4:

Speaker A: *Some of my friends always insist on buying designer clothes but I don't think they are getting good value for money.*

Speaker B: *I always buy clothes with a famous name. I like to look good when I go out.*

Speaker A: *Okay, but do you really think they're worth paying more for?*

Speaker B: *And I wouldn't dream of being seen in trainers from one of those cheap street markets.*

Speaker A: *Um… right. But as I said before, I have my doubts that clothes or shoes that cost five times as much as the cheaper options are actually five times better quality.*

Speaker B: *You can always tell when somebody is wearing fake clothes.*

This is a short dialogue about the subject of designer goods (List A). Speaker B has broken one of the most important rules of conversation - she has not asked any questions. Although we frequently have a lot to say about various issues, in a genuine dialogue you must take turns with your interlocutor and you must show that you are interested in what they are saying by asking them questions to gather more information. Simply expressing your point of view without doing this is **not** a conversation.

Not only has Speaker B not asked Speaker A any questions, she also ignored (or did not hear) the question that Speaker A asked her. This is additional evidence that she is not actively engaged in listening.

MAKING COMMENTS

Conversation 5 uses the same prompt as Conversation 4:

Speaker A: *Some of my friends always insist on buying designer clothes but I don't think they are getting good value for money.*

Speaker B: *Really? Well, I always buy clothes with a famous name. But why don't you think they're worth it?*

Speaker A: *For a start, just because they have a designer label on them doesn't mean to say that they are going to last longer, or that they're better quality.*

Speaker B: *Okay, I see what you're saying but I can't agree with you. I've bought cheap clothes in the past and they fall apart much faster - and the colours fade, too.*

Speaker A: *I have to admit that I bought a pair of really expensive designer shoes fifteen years ago and they're still in great condition. But don't you think they charge far too much for what you're actually buying?*

Speaker B: *No, not really. I mean, you're paying for something that has been designed by talented people and made with top quality materials. Don't you think that's worth paying more for?*

You can see that in this conversation, Speaker B is responding to the questions that she is asked. More than this, she is making comments that are relevant to what Speaker A is saying - "I've bought cheap clothes in the past and they fall apart much faster…" and "…you're paying for something that has been designed by talented people…". Making relevant comments like this will encourage the other person to respond, add structure to the conversation and allow it to flow more freely.

LANGUAGE FUNCTIONS

If you have already been practicing the GESE 10 interactive phase, you should be familiar with the concept of language functions. In this section, you will find information similar to that available in the companion volume to this one, **Trinity GESE 10 Interactive Phase.** However, the sample conversations reflect the subjects from List A and List B.

So, what are language functions? Putting it simply, they are the different ways in which we put grammar, vocabulary and pronunciation together in our daily lives in order to communicate with other people. Basic language functions include asking questions, agreeing, disagreeing and expressing preferences.

In the Trinity GESE examinations, language functions are cumulative - in other words, you are expected to be able to use all of the ones from preceding levels. If you have doubts about what is required, look at the criteria for GESE Levels 7-9 available online. For GESE 10 there are five specific language functions that you need to demonstrate and these are what we are going to look at now in more detail.

DEVELOPING AN ARGUMENT

When you develop an argument, you need to present a convincing case by providing evidence to support what you are saying and by giving examples. You might have to do this for a number of reasons, such as when somebody has challenged your beliefs or if they are not sure about what you are saying.

You should also be prepared to provide supporting information because giving a simple reason for what you are saying is rarely going to be sufficient:

List A: Communication.

Speaker A: I can understand why parents are so worried that their children are losing the ability to communicate. Just look at all the emojis and abbreviations they're using in their text messages these days.

*Speaker B: Ok, **let me explain my point of view. For a start**, I don't think there is any evidence to suggest that texting is destroying our ability to have face-to-face conversations. If that was happening, the world would be a very quiet place and it clearly isn't!*

Speaker A: Ok, I take your point but I've heard examples of young people using text abbreviations in essays.

*Speaker B: Well, that might happen occasionally but I'm sure it's not such a huge problem as people think it is. **For another thing,** I think text messaging has actually improved communication in some ways because it's instant. **What's more**, young people aren't as irresponsible as adults try to say they are. They're still getting good grades in languages, for example.*

Other ways of developing an argument are to introduce your additional points with the following phrases:

What's more, it's my opinion/belief that…
Then again, I think that…
And in addition…
Oh, and another thing is that…
Something else I'd like to say is…
While on the subject, I think that…

DEFENDING A POINT OF VIEW

Sometimes, you might be directly challenged by somebody who wants you to justify your point of view. This can happen because they do not agree with you, or because they don't think you have sufficient knowledge of the subject you are discussing, or perhaps they feel that you lack experience.

In an exam situation, hesitating when challenged can mean the difference between passing and failing:

List B: Stress management.

Speaker A: How can you say that stress at work is affecting the economy?

*Speaker B: **I'm sure I'm right about this because** there are statistics to prove that hundreds of thousands of working hours are lost every year due to stress.*

Speaker A: Hmm. I'm not sure if I believe in statistics. In any case, are you sure it isn't just people deciding to take a couple of days off every now and then?

*Speaker B: **Actually, there's more to it than that.** The experts say that stress is a serious problem and it can have really negative long term effects on people if it isn't treated.*

Here are some other useful phrases for defending your point of view:

I'm pretty positive because…
Let me justify my point of view…
In defense of this, I'd like to say…
I have to respond to that because…
I'm quite certain about this because...

EXPRESSING BELIEFS

Always state clearly the degree to which you do and do not believe something. Of course, there are many levels of certainty and uncertainty and it is perfectly acceptable to say that you neither agree nor disagree about something as long as you can be clear about your intention and maintain the conversation at the same time:

List A: Roles in the family.

Speaker A: *So, you think that grandparents should be paid for looking after their grandchildren?*

Speaker B: *Oh, **I'm absolutely certain about that.** Most grandparents have worked hard all their lives and are retired, but then they're expected to take care of the grandkids for sometimes nine or ten hours a day. It simply isn't fair.*

Speaker A: *Well… that's because parents have to go out to work and they often can't pay for professional childcare so they have no other option, do they?*

Speaker B: *Sorry, but I'm not going to change my mind about this. **I definitely think that** if grandparents are expected to take on the role of carers, they should receive some kind of official payment from the Government.*

Here is a selection of other useful phrases for expressing strong beliefs and more tentative ones:

I strongly believe that…
It's my firm belief that…
I couldn't be more certain that…
It's obvious to everybody that…
I'm fairly certain that…

I'm pretty sure that…
To my way of thinking…
Don't you agree with me about..?
I just can't believe that…
I'm afraid I can't accept that…

EXPRESSING OPINIONS TENTATIVELY

It is frequently a good idea to express your beliefs in a clear and direct way, but you can also say what you are thinking in a more tentative manner (or more indirectly) when you are not sure about your point of view, or you do not know much about the topic of conversation.

Giving tentative opinions can also be useful to avoid upsetting somebody or making them angry if you are discussing a controversial or sensitive subject about which another person might have strong opinions. If you can do this, it may take the focus of criticism away from yourself. It is always sensible not to assume that another person shares your views and that they might object if you attempt to impose your opinions upon them.

List B: The future of the planet.

Speaker A: Our planet is in a terrible situation and it's all due to fossil fuels. There's only one solution - we must prohibit their use within the next twenty years.

Speaker B: Oh, well... **I'm not saying it's my opinion but** *some people would say that's a bit of an unrealistic goal.* **I may be wrong, but** *I'm not sure if we have the technology to achieve that in such a short space of time.*

Speaker A: I'm afraid I don't really agree with that opinion. We have had clea, green technology for years - you know, electric cars, wind and solar energy. We've had more than enough time to adjust. So why hasn't the world stopped using oil and gas?

Speaker B: **I'm not sure I have all the answers to that** *but there must be some scientific and economic reasons… (etcetera).*

Additional phrases for expressing opinions tentatively include:

Well, I may be wrong but…
Correct me if I'm wrong but…
Some people think that…
I'm not sure but it's possible that…
I tend to agree with other people when they say…
I'm no expert, but don't you think..?
I'm not sure if I'm right about this, but…

SUMMARISING INFORMATION, IDEAS AND ARGUMENTS

Summarising what somebody else has said is a useful way of checking that you have understood them because it gives them the opportunity to correct you if you are wrong. It also demonstrates that you are listening, and it can be a useful way of bringing the conversation to an end. Remember that you can also summarise what **you** have said to clarify your point.

List A: Use of the internet.

Speaker A: Something that worries me a lot is the amount of fake information on the internet. I mean, I know there are restrictions and everything but they're really not enough, are they? I believe in freedom of speech, but not if it's going to damage the health and wellbeing of lots of people. It's time that more money was provided by the international community to come up with coordinated solutions to the problem.

*Speaker B: **So what you're saying is** there should be some kind of international organisation to combat fake information on the internet. **Is that right?***

Speaker A: Yes, something like that. It's a global problem so we need to work together to deal with it.

Speaker B: I understand what you're saying.

Here are some more ways that you can summarise or ask somebody to summarise:

All in all, I'd say that…
At the end of the day…
Putting it in a nutshell…
If I understand right, what you're saying is…
To simplify things, what you're saying is…
To wrap it up, I'd say that…

DEDUCING

In conversations, people often do not provide us with direct information. In situations like this, we need to reach a conclusion based on the evidence that they give us:

List B: International events.

Speaker A: I'd like to take more interest in big international events like all these conferences on the global economy but I find it really difficult.

Speaker B: Oh? Why is that?

Speaker A: Well, you know, all that technical language about money and stuff like that… it doesn't make any sense and it's so boring. I'm sure it's really important, though. I mean, it affects the lives of everybody on the planet. We have international organisations that should be doing more to educate ordinary people like you and me.

*Speaker B: **So what you're saying is,** people like the World Bank and the United Nations should make economic issues more easy to understand for the general public?*

Speaker A: Exactly.

Other phrases to indicate that you are going to deduce something from the information you have been given are:

I gather from what you're saying…
Putting two and two together, I'd say…
Weighing all the evidence up…
So, what I get from everything you're saying is...
I think that what you're trying to say is that…
I reckon that what you mean is…

Before we take a look at the language functions for GESE Grade 9, a final note on how to use those for Grade 10. Do not forget that you may have to talk about people in the third person, and that the examiner will also be using these functions. Functional language will apply equally in these situations. For example, you can deduce information about a person who is not actually present in the conversation:

Speaker A: *I've asked my brother if he would help me move house next week but he keeps coming up with different excuses and to be honest they're not convincing… you know, one minute he needs to get his car fixed, the next he's got an important project to finish for university. His attitude is really annoying me.*

Speaker B: *So maybe he just doesn't want to help you?*

TRINITY GESE GRADE 9 LANGUAGE FUNCTIONS

The language functions for Trinity GESE examinations are **cumulative**. It is therefore a very good idea to make sure you know what those at lower levels are (for example, levels 7, 8 and 9) and how to use them. I have included here a list of the level 9 functions and some examples:

EXPRESSING ABSTRACT IDEAS

It is sometimes hard to explain a difficult concept or idea in a direct way so it might be necessary to tell a story or to compare something complicated with something familiar (for example; "imagine the layers of the atmosphere as if they were the rings of an onion…"). You can introduce these ideas with phrases such as:

Try and imagine that…
Let's look at it this way…
It's difficult to understand so let me explain it this way…

EXPRESSING REGRETS, WISHES AND HOPES

Talking about our past regrets and future hopes and wishes, and asking questions about them, are fundamental parts of the human experience:

If only she hadn't…
Do you sometimes wish you had..?
I really hope that…
Do you ever wish you could..?
I really think I shouldn't have…
I'd like to think that in the future I could...

EXPRESSING ASSUMPTIONS

Although you always need to base your interactions during the interactive phase on the evidence you have obtained through your questions, sometimes it can be useful to make assumptions to move the conversation on or to help the other person clarify what they are saying due to hesitation or uncertainty:

Well, I assume that…
I guess that…
It's best to assume that…
I've no doubt that…
I'm pretty certain that...

PARAPHRASING

Paraphrasing what another person has said to you - putting it into your own words - is a good way to check that you have understood, and also demonstrates that you are listening to them:

So, what you're saying is…
I guess that what you're telling me is…
So, putting it in other words you could say that...

EVALUATING OPTIONS

Instead of simply coming up with one solution, it demonstrates an ability to think in a more creative and flexible manner if you are able to consider the different aspects of several possibilities, positive, negative and neutral:

On one hand, you could…
Alternatively, you might want to…
There's a lot to be said for (A but (B) might also work...
While (A) is probably the best idea, (B) has a few advantages over it...

HYPOTHESISING

When we hypothesise about the possible outcome of an action, it shows that we can think and express ourselves in a more creative manner. This demonstrates an ability for advanced problem solving:

I imagine that if you…
It should be possible to, at least in theory…
If you…
I reckon that if you tried that,…

EVALUATING PAST ACTIONS OR COURSE OF EVENTS

Talking about the success or failure of past actions is just as important as hypothesising about the potential outcomes of those in the future. This can help to clarify what might or might not work again if you are asked to give advice:

I suppose you wish you had…
I guess that wasn't such a good idea…
All in all, that worked out pretty well…
It's worth remembering that for the future…
At the end of the day the results weren't too good because…
If we'd done it a different way, it might have turned out better...

GRAMMAR

There are no specific grammar requirements for GESE Grade 10 but a very good knowledge of C1 grammar is essential. Candidates must be able to express complex ideas, avoid misunderstanding and put across concepts in different ways.

To achieve this, your use of grammar needs to be confident and consistent throughout the examination. Although there are ways that you can give yourself time to think about how you are going to respond to a question or comment in situations where you are uncertain about what to say, you do not have enough time to carefully construct a phrase if you are not sure about the grammar you need to use.

If you are not confident that you can achieve this, you should **not** think about taking the exam until you have reviewed all areas of English grammar at C1 level . To do this, you can take a look at the requirements for the Common European Framework of Reference for C1 (you can easily find this information on the internet). There are few books specific to Trinity English examinations that provide a complete guide to the recommended grammar but fortunately there are plenty of good grammar books available for this level.

In short, you need to revise the grammar thoroughly. Make sure that you can confidently use all of the past, present and future verb tenses in a conversation. An ability to use abstract language and to evaluate hypothetical situations is important at this level so you must have more than a theoretical knowledge of conditional structures (including third and mixed conditionals) along with past modals for expressing certainty and uncertainty.

LEXIS

What is lexis? Putting it simply, this word is used in the study of linguistics to describe the vocabulary of a language or the aspects of the language other than the grammar.

Trinity GESE 10 tests your skills to communicate with spoken English at CEFR (Common European Framework of Reference) level C1, for which you are expected to have an extensive knowledge of vocabulary. This is more than just a matter of "knowing nouns" - it means you have to be confident with using nouns, adjectives, verbs and adverbs in different combinations such as collocations and compound nouns, and for a wide range of purposes.

At this level, you are also expected to be familiar with how idioms (fixed phrases which are widely understood by English speakers) and metaphors are used. You need to demonstrate to the examiner that you can speak easily, naturally and creatively about a wide variety of topics.

There is no "instant fix" to improving your vocabulary, but words and phrases are useless if you do not use them. Don't be afraid to experiment and do not be scared of making mistakes - mistakes are among the most useful of all learning tools as long as we learn from them.

If you are not sure if you have a C1 level of vocabulary, try this simple exercise. Find a variety of reading texts for C1 English examinations (you will find examples of the ISE III reading and writing examinations on the official Trinity website) and study them, underlining any vocabulary including single words and phrases that you do not understand. This can provide you with an indication of whether or not you need to work at improving your lexical knowhow.

PHONOLOGY

Phonology is the science of speech sounds. Natural, spoken English is filled with variations of inflexion, intonation and stress in the same way as your own native language and it is important to demonstrate it confidently at GESE Level 10. Listening regularly to native speakers will help you to identify these patterns.

Why is phonology such an important part of the GESE 10 evaluation? Above all, spoken language must sound natural. It is not only the words that demonstrate the nuances of emotion and depth of opinion: much of what we communicate to others is contained in the way our speech sounds. Above all, you must avoid using monotonous or "robotic" speech because this conveys negative information such as nervousness or lack of engagement in the conversation.

There are a number of general aspects of phonology that you need to be aware of.

One of these is **intonation**. Notice how a speaker's voice rises to introduce a new idea and falls to indicate the conclusion:

(Rising intonation): And now, the headlines. Hurricane Daisy has caused widespread damage throughout the Caribbean with up to five hundred homes destroyed and electricity supplies seriously disrupted. Fortunately, there are so far no reports of serious injury, although rescue teams are working in the region to reach remote islands and communities. (Falling intonation): Heavy rain is expected to keep falling until at least the weekend.

(Rising intonation): In Sydney, Australia, the next round of climate talks are due to start this afternoon. It is expected that there will be major opposition to some of the proposals from the major industrialised countries but … (etcetera)

Stressing key words is also important to communicate feelings and emphasis. In order to do this, we often put stress on words such as adjectives and adverbs:

Honestly! _I had been looking forward to seeing that film for weeks but the experience was_ _completely ruined_ _by the family in front of me. I've_ _never_ _seen such_ _badly behaved_ _children. They were laughing and throwing popcorn all over the place… it was_ _disgusting!_ _Personally, I blame the parents._

As I said earlier, when expressing strong ideas, emotions and empathy, you **must not** speak in a monotone. Remember that the interactive task is roleplay and you need to imagine that the situation is real.

While stressing adjectives and adverbs in this way is important to give your speech more colour, so is the correct stress on syllables in longer and more complex words. For example, the stress in the following words is placed on the syllable before the suffix: am<u>bi</u>tious, com<u>mer</u>cial, navi<u>ga</u>tion. In some other words, the stress is placed on the third to last syllable: u<u>na</u>nimous, a<u>ty</u>pical, ri<u>di</u>culous.

However, you should also be aware that some words have a weak form when they are not used at the beginning of a sentence. These words include _for, can, and, had, of, a, an, are, has, of_ and _at. Go and get me a coffee, please_, for example, is typically pronounced _Go/n/get me a coffee, please_, while _I can come and help you in the garden tomorrow_ becomes _I/cn come/n help you in the garden tomorrow._

The speed at which we talk can also carry important information. When we slow down, it might convey that we are uncertain about our opinion or that we want to express caution. On the other hand, if you want to suggest certainty or urgency, you will often speak more rapidly. Remember, however, that in the exam speaking too quickly can also suggest that you are nervous **and** it can make you more difficult to understand.

THE IMPORTANCE OF "UM", "RIGHT", "WELL" AND "UH-HUH"

A frequent problem that is encountered when attempting to develop more natural conversation for many students of English is that they have only been taught how to use formal grammar in writing and speech, and that colourful, colloquial language and idioms should not be used. Worse still, they are often discouraged from using these expressions in the mistaken idea that they are somehow "wrong".

While formal language might be appropriate when writing an essay, report or letter of application or when giving a presentation, during natural conversation the opposite is generally the case. One of the requirements at Trinity GESE Grade 10 is for you to be aware of these nuances of English and to be able to use them with confidence.

For example, you need to show the other person that you are paying attention. Apart from paying attention to your interlocutor and using appropriate body language such as smiles and nods, the use of sounds like "uhum" and "mmm" and words like "right" and "I see" demonstrates that you are interested in the conversation.

What is more, a well-placed "well", "you know" or "I guess that" punctuates your conversation, helps to avoid uncomfortable silences and gives you and the other person time to think about what you are going to say next.

Read these two versions of the same paragraph aloud. Which of them sounds most natural?

1. *I started writing when I was ten years old and I had my first short story published in the school magazine when I was thirteen. It was a scary story for Halloween but I do not remember the name. Yes, I do. It was called "The Shadow in the Cellar". My parents were very proud of me but it was a bit embarrassing when my teacher made me read the story to the rest of the class. If I remember correctly, I was seventeen when I started work on a novel but it was not very good*

and by that time I was getting ready to go to university so it was years later that I had time to start writing again. I never imagined that my first book would be such a success.

2. *Er… well, I started writing when I was… um… about ten years old and I had my first short story published in the school magazine when I was… erm… thirteen. Yeah, thirteen. It was a scary story for Halloween and it was called - hold on a moment, what was it? Oh yes! "The Shadow in the Cellar". You know, my parents were really proud of me but, well, it was a bit embarrassing when my teacher made me read it to the rest of the class, I can tell you! Anyways, I think I was about seventeen when I started writing a novel but… well, to be honest it wasn't very good and by then I was getting ready for university so it was years later that I had time to start writing again. You know, I never imagined that my first book would be such a success!*

TRINITY GESE 10 CONVERSATION LIST A

The Trinity GESE Conversation Phase List A consists of subjects that are generally considered to be more suitable for younger candidates. However, it should be remembered that the same level of English is required to succeed in both List A and List B.

Each list of questions is introduced by a general introduction which is intended to promote active thinking and discussion about the subject. Please note that the questions are intended for practice and do not necessarily reflect the full range of themes that you might be asked about in the examination.

A useful exercise is to write down as many of your own ideas as you can think of for each subject. You can then come up with questions for each idea and practice asking and answering them in a classroom setting or with a native English speaker.

ROLES IN THE FAMILY

The roles that different members of our families play can vary considerably for many reasons. In some countries, traditional roles related to gender are still central to family life, while in other parts of the world the situation has become more flexible over the last few decades.

One of these changes is the increasing number of families in which both parents have full time jobs. This sometimes means that grandparents or other members of the extended family are taking more responsibility for childcare. However, in some cultures and societies, grandparents have always played a central role in looking after the younger family members.

Changing family dynamics have also affected the responsibilities of teenagers and young adults, many of whom need to become more independent at an earlier age. Sometimes the opposite is true, however, with greater competition for jobs meaning that some young people cannot afford to move out of the family home until their late twenties or thirties.

1. I am concerned that families with young children are relying more and more on grandparents for childcare.

2. Do you think that fathers should be given the same amount of paternity leave as mothers have maternity leave?

3. Teenagers should be doing a lot more to help with household chores like cooking and cleaning.

4. When I was a child, my father used to do most of the cooking. Do you think that women and men are better at different household tasks? Why/why not?

5. Parents are usually expected to be good role models for their children but this does not always happen.

6. It is often said that a traditional family structure with two parents is best for children. What is your opinion about this?

7. Little girls are often dressed in pink and given dolls to play with while little boys wear blue and have toy guns and trucks. I wonder if this behaviour can encourage gender stereotypes?

8. How do you think the roles of different family members are going to change in the future?

9. Should children be expected to care for their parents when they get old?

10. Do you think that our best friends can be a part of our family or do families only consist of our relatives?

COMMUNICATION

Since the start of the computer and internet age, the way in which we communicate has changed beyond recognition. Only a little over a hundred years ago, if we wanted to talk to somebody on the other side of the world we had to write a letter that could take weeks or even months to reach them: now, we can send a text message or email that reaches its destination almost instantly.

But how has this communication revolution affected mankind? Has it all been good news or has it created new problems? There are many different opinions about this. New technology has certainly made knowledge far more widely available but some people worry that we are losing our ability to have real conversations. Others think that we are becoming more impatient so that nowadays we say that we do not have time to read books, articles and newspapers. On the other hand, e-books are widely available and with its instant, free access, the internet allows us to browse through the greatest library of information that has ever existed.

1. Many children nowadays don't even know how to write a letter or an email. This is a big problem.

2. I wonder if there are too many TV channels nowadays. Many of them are of very poor quality.

3. Politicians are bad at communicating with the public. Maybe this is the reason why so many people are not interested in politics.

4. Do you think that there should be a single global language? Why/why not?

5. I frequently see groups of friends sitting together but they aren't talking to each other because they are using their mobile phones.

6. If you were not able to speak, what do you think would be the best way of communicating with other people?

7. How important do you think different types of non-verbal communication such as body language and facial expressions are?

8. I think that the quality of verbal communication is deteriorating because we have forgotten how to listen to each other.

9. Do you think that young people are interested in what is happening in the news?

10. What do you think is the most important aspect of learning a new language?

THE SCHOOL CURRICULUM

There is much debate among students, teachers and parents about whether the school curriculum adequately prepares young people for the responsibilities of adult life and future professions.

While the range of subjects available in schools has diversified to include themes related to technology and innovation, much criticism remains regarding the importance of traditional subjects and the use of outdated teaching methods. Some education authorities have taken steps both to include practical life skills and vocational subjects in the curriculum and to change the way in which students are evaluated, with less reliance on examination results and more importance attached to project work and continual assessment.

Despite this, even primary school children often have to take frequent and demanding tests and some educationalists believe this system does not truly evaluate the performance and potential of young people.

1. I sometimes wonder if children are being made to study far too many subjects at school.

2. It is a pity that creative subjects such as art, music and drama are not a more important part of the school curriculum.

3. Do you think that high class numbers of twenty five or thirty affect the ability to learn?

4. Should it be obligatory to learn more than one foreign language at school? Why/why not?

5. Do you think that parents should be permitted to educate their children at home?

6. Because some children do not like playing team sports, these should be optional activities at school.

7. If you could choose, what new subjects would you add to the school curriculum?

8. In some countries, young people have to attend extra classes in the evening after they finish school. What do you think about this?

9. I think that more secondary students would be interested in school if the curriculum included practical subjects like car mechanics, gardening and catering.

10. Exams don't really assess the individual progress of students. There must be a better way of evaluating their performance.

YOUTH BEHAVIOUR

Many stereotypes exist regarding young people and some adults have fixed ideas about the behaviour of teenagers in particular. But are these frequently negative portrayals justified?

In recent years, increasing numbers of young people have been at the forefront of campaigns to combat climate change and social injustices. Others have inspired older generations with achievements in the fields of sport, fashion, literature and art. At the same time, crime and antisocial behaviour among adolescents continues to be a problem in some sectors of society. There are many theories put forward to explain this, including lack of parental control, lack of resources for young people, failure of governments to involve young people in the decision-making processes which affect their lives and issues such as poverty and unemployment.

1. Many young people prefer to stay at home and use the internet instead of meeting with friends or playing sports. I think this is a serious problem.

2. It is unfair that so many adults have a negative opinion about teenage behaviour when they did similar things when they were young.

3. I am very encouraged to see how many young people are becoming involved in action to help society and protect the environment.

4. Perhaps one reason for bad behaviour among some young people is the lack of facilities for them such as youth and sports clubs.

5. Do you think that politicians should consult young people before making decisions that affect their lives - for example, changes to the education system?

6. At what age do you think young people should be allowed to leave school and find a job?

7. It can sometimes be difficult to encourage teenagers to eat healthy food. I wonder what can be done about this.

8. Bullying at school and online affects the lives of many young people. We need to do far more to prevent it from happening.

9. In what ways are your hobbies and free time activities different to those of your parents when they were young?

10. Should people under the age of eighteen be sent to prison if they commit a crime?

USE OF THE INTERNET

Ask people what they think is the greatest technological achievement of the last fifty years and the majority will say 'the invention of the internet'. It has changed our lives so radically that we cannot imagine a world without it. But although we rely on the internet for everything from education and banking to entertainment and shopping, it continues to generate strong opinions, both positive and negative.

One particularly controversial matter is the increasing use of social networking. Many parents worry about the risks to their children caused by cyberbullying and lack of confidentiality. On the other hand, social networks can bring people with similar interests together and help create friendships. Other concerns include fake information and extremist websites. On the other hand, resources such as Wikipedia provide us with information about any subject at the click of a button.

1. Some people believe that young children should not be allowed to use the internet. What do you think?

2. I don't think that buying things online is as much fun as going to the shops.

3. Many websites include false information which can be very dangerous. More should be done to prevent this from happening but I'm not sure how.

4. Should the internet be free for everybody to use?

5. In the future, all school and university subjects might be taught online. What do you think about this?

6. Can you think of any ways in which the internet has influenced our lives in a negative way?

7. Many people download films and music from the internet without paying for them. Do you think that more should be done to prevent this activity?

8. Young people spend so much time online that they are not reading books anymore.

9. How much time every day do you think that parents should permit their children to use the internet?

10.   How do you think that social networking sites like Facebook and Instagram could be improved?

DESIGNER GOODS

Are expensive designer products worth paying more money for? Famous name clothes, perfumes and beauty products are generally thought to be of better quality than cheap alternatives, but how do we know if this is really true?

Some famous clothes manufacturers have been criticised for using cheap labour in developing countries. Despite this, other exclusive fashion companies produce limited numbers of quality garments and other accessories but sell them at a very high price. Supporters of the fashion industry say that they are providing a service that consumers want and that wearing the most fashionable items helps people to feel good about themselves. Nevertheless, designers are criticised for using materials that rely on the exploitation of animals or cause damage to the environment.

1. I don't think that the prices charged for designer-labelled goods are justified.

2. Do you think that there is a difference between real designer goods and imitations?

3. How do designer goods benefit the economy?

4. What product would you be most prepared to buy for its designer label?

5. Some top fashion labels use cheap labour in developing countries to manufacture their products. How do you feel about this?

6. If somebody wears expensive designer clothes and accessories, does that change your opinion of that person?

7. I do not understand why many well-known beauty products and perfumes are so expensive. Why do you think this is?

8. Some people say that they would never buy second hand clothes and accessories, even if they were of excellent quality. What is your opinion about this?

9. I think that we need to do more to help young designers set up their own businesses.

10. Is it wrong to exploit animals in order to produce expensive fur coats and leather handbags?

TRINITY GESE GRADE 10 CONVERSATION LIST B

The Trinity GESE Conversation Phase List B consists of subjects that are generally considered to be more suitable for adult candidates. However, it should be remembered that the same level of English is required to succeed in both List A and List B.

Each list of questions is introduced by a general introduction which is intended to promote active thinking and discussion about the subject. Please note that the questions are intended for practice and do not necessarily reflect the full range of themes that you might be asked about in the examination.

A useful exercise is to write down as many of your own ideas as you can think of for each subject. You can then come up with questions for each idea and practice asking and answering them in a classroom setting or with a native English speaker.

INTERNATIONAL EVENTS

When we think about the different categories of international events, sports competitions such as the Olympic and Commonwealth Games are frequently at the top of the list. There are many others, such as the Wimbledon and US Open tennis championships, the Tour de France cycle race and the football World Cup.

These, however, are not the only international events which attract participants. In the world of culture and music, there are competitions such as Eurovision and world music festivals like Womad, while cinema has the Cannes Film festival. Furthermore, there are awards ceremonies including the Oscars and, in Spain, the Goyas.

It is important to remember that when we talk about international events, we do not only mean sports competitions and festivals related to the arts. Conferences are held by the G7 and G20 international economic organisations, and in recent years the United Nations has convened climate action summits in an attempt to improve international cooperation to combat environmental problems.

1. I often wonder how we can encourage the public to take more interest in international conferences on the economy and the environment.

2. It is sometimes claimed that events like the Olympic Games promote understanding and cooperation between nations but I don't see any evidence of this.

3. It is a pity that there are not more international music festivals and competitions. I'm sure the public would be very interested in this.

4. International cinema awards are too heavily focused on English language films. This means that films made in other languages are always at a disadvantage.

5. Is it more important to learn about international historical events that have shaped the whole world or the history of individual countries?

6. Some regional events like the US Presidential Elections have become events of international interest and importance. Why do you think this has happened?

7. The United Nations has designated dozens of International Days to raise awareness about issues ranging from deforestation and particular illnesses, to commemorations of important events in history. Do you think this is a good idea?

8. Some countries are trying to promote their traditional festivals as international tourist attractions. Do you think this will have a positive or a negative effect on local communities?

9. The enormous amounts of money spent on large sporting events cannot be justified when there is so much poverty and suffering in the world.

10. Do you think that countries which abuse human rights should be prohibited from participating in global sports competitions and cultural festivals?

EQUAL OPPORTUNITIES

A discussion about equal opportunities may include issues such as access to employment and education that are related to gender, ability, ethnicity and financial means, among others. Many nations have passed laws in an attempt to make sure that all citizens have the same rights, but how effective are these laws in reality?

For example, the cost of university education varies widely depending on the country. Where university fees are particularly high, this might prevent young people from poorer families from accessing higher education.

Another issue is that of gender rights in employment. Even where legislation exists to protect employees, there are still examples of companies discriminating against women who plan to have a family.

1. Although older people are generally very experienced, it is frequently difficult for them to find work again if they lose their jobs.

2. Perhaps it would be a good idea to encourage more women to enter traditionally male professions, and vice versa.

3. I think that it is completely wrong to employ individuals just because of their physical appearance or style.

4. Even though young people usually have more energy and motivation, they frequently encounter serious problems when trying to enter the job market.

5. Despite laws to prevent discrimination in the workplace, we still hear about cases of individuals from ethnic minorities who have their job applications rejected.

6. It is often claimed that higher education is accessible to everybody but with the cost of doing a university degree rising all the time this simply is not true.

7. With regards to disabilities, total equality in the workplace is a completely unrealistic goal.

8. Should the most gifted and talented students be given special treatment at school?

9. Compared with other people, the members of hereditary monarchies and the aristocracy are automatically at an advantage. Therefore, countries that have them can never claim to provide equal opportunities to everybody.

10.   Many employers have a policy of positive discrimination, which means they have to employ a certain percentage of disabled workers and individuals from different ethnic groups. Do you think this policy is an effective way of promoting equal opportunities?

SOCIAL ISSUES

Despite huge improvements in standards of living and healthcare provision during the last one hundred years, it would seem that on a global basis, inequality is greater than ever. Even in wealthy countries such as the USA and the United Kingdom, the gap between rich and poor continues to grow and the number of people regarded as living on or below the poverty line is of great concern. In developing countries, millions of people still live in absolute poverty.

Social issues and problems have many causes, of course. Poverty and lack of access to education can result in poor housing and sanitation, increased levels of crime and limited access to hospitals. Other situations that affect people's lives include climate change (which can have a dramatic effect on food and water supplies) and armed conflicts.

1. What can we do to reduce the level of crime in cities?

2. Providing aid to developing countries is often left to charities or non government organisations. I don't think this is right.

3. Countries around the world need to be more tolerant towards both legal and illegal immigrants.

4. It is not possible to provide universal, free healthcare for everybody. Private health plans are therefore the best option.

5. Why do so many people around the world still not have access to clean drinking water and other basic necessities?

6. Youth unemployment is rising all through the western world. Why do you think this is?

7. I think that our elderly population is well looked after by the State but some people do not agree with me.

8. Do you think that house prices should be controlled by city councils?

9. We are never going to solve the problem of homelessness because some people actually refuse to live in social housing and prefer to live on the streets instead.

10. Although a high standard of living and level of wellbeing is generally associated with higher salaries, there are some non-materialistic societies around the world where the members are very happy. I think that we can learn a lot from them.

THE FUTURE OF THE PLANET

Never before has human activity had such a profound impact on the planet. The majority of climate scientists agree that mankind is the cause of the increasing rate of climate change, although there are still climate change deniers who claim that any change is a natural process.

Not only are global weather patterns altering but we are also losing ecosystems and animal plant species at a worrying rate. In addition, the oceans are suffering from pollution and are the destination of vast quantities of plastic that enters the food chain and ultimately ends up in our own bodies.

These factors are going to have a profound effect on our future. What will Planet Earth be like in 50 years time? Will we find solutions to the problems facing us? Are electric cars going to completely replace vehicles that depend on fossil fuels? How will rising sea levels affect the millions of people who live in coastal cities? These and many other challenges remain to be overcome.

1. When I think about what life might be like in fifty years time, I feel very pessimistic.

2. We depend on ecosystems and all other species of plants and animals for our own survival. If we do not do more to protect them, the human species is not going to survive.

3. How will we provide enough energy to maintain our modern lifestyle when the oil, coal and gas run out?

4. Sea levels are rising and this process is predicted to speed up in the future. What can we do to help the millions of people who live in coastal areas?

5. It is predicted that in the future most of the population will live in mega-cities and rural areas will become depopulated. What do you think about this?

6. What can we do to increase society's awareness of the need to separate waste for recycling?

7. The global population continues to rise exponentially and could reach almost 9 billion by 2030. How will the world feed so many people?

8. Although climate change is usually considered to be exclusively negative, some of the consequences might actually be quite beneficial for us.

9. If we all stopped eating meat, greenhouse gases would be dramatically reduced. In fact, if everybody adopted a vegan diet, this would go a long way to saving the planet.

10. A world without iconic species such as tigers, elephants and rhinos would be a very depressing place but these animals are disappearing fast and we are not doing enough to protect them.

SCIENTIFIC DEVELOPMENTS

Science and innovation has benefited mankind in countless ways, but have all scientific achievements been positive for us? The work of scientists and inventors has provided us with sources of energy, cures for many illnesses and rapid transport but has also created dangerous weapons and industrial processes that contribute to pollution and climate change.

Increasingly, the world is looking to science to overcome challenges from how to feed a growing global population to finding innovative new uses for the rubbish we throw away. But are we doing enough to support the next generation of scientists by providing the best university degrees and money for research? In addition, many branches of science and investigation - among them, genetic modification and space exploration - are controversial with strong opinions both in favour of and against them.

1. Not including the internet or the mobile phone, which invention of the last century do you think has had the greatest impact on our lives?

2. Perhaps the world should spend more money on developing medical treatments and vaccines than improving information technology.

3. There has been a lot of debate recently about the benefits and dangers of artificial intelligence. Personally, I am not sure what I think about this subject.

4. The role of women in contributing to scientific breakthroughs has long been ignored because it has traditionally been assumed that all scientists are men.

5. How can we encourage more young people to become scientists?

6. We often think of scientific achievements as modern events but the truth is that many major discoveries in the fields of mathematics,

astronomy and physics were made thousands of years ago. I wonder why we have forgotten about these pioneers?

7. There are many scientific achievements and inventions that mankind would be much better off without.

8. I think that space exploration is a complete waste of time and money. Science should be focused exclusively on resolving the many problems we have on our own planet.

9. Genetic engineering of human beings is considered a taboo subject but I am not sure why. Just think of how much stronger, more intelligent and resistant to diseases we could be if this type of research was permitted.

10.   What types of technology would you like to see in the house of the future?

STRESS MANAGEMENT

Stress is one of the major causes of absence from work and can be a sign of underlying physical and mental health problems. Some companies have introduced programmes to increase the happiness and general wellbeing of their staff. Even so, employers and even the medical profession sometimes downplay the serious consequences of stress and suffers who take time off work are sometimes negatively labelled as being lazy or inefficient.

Of course, there are many other reasons for suffering stress, but it seems that whatever the cause, we are not very good at managing it. While there are some very effective and healthy ways of reducing stress levels, many resort to unhealthy behaviours in an attempt to get rid of it which only result in making the problem worse.

1. So many people are stressed these days but in general doctors do not give their patients enough help in managing the problem.

2. I have been feeling very anxious at work recently but I don't know what to do about it.

3. One of the biggest causes of stress is when companies and businesses make their employees work very long hours without sufficient breaks.

4. It is a pity nowadays that we don't talk to each other enough about our problems. If we did, this would go a long way to reducing our stress levels.

5. A lot of people try to reduce their stress levels with medication, alcohol and other substances. What do you think about this?

6. Personally, I don't know why everybody seems to complain about stress. A little bit of pressure is good for you.

7. Nowadays, even primary school students are forced to take regular exams. I am not surprised, therefore, that so many young people are suffering from psychological problems.

8. What advice would you give to a friend or relative who was suffering from stress?

9. Relaxation techniques and therapies like yoga, massage and meditation can be very effective in reducing stress. Should the public health service provide them free of charge?

10. A lot of stress is the result of trying to do too much. I believe that learning how to spend time doing absolutely nothing can really help us disconnect from our problems.

Other books available from Amazon by the same author:

TRINITY GESE GRADE 10 LISTENING PHASE
TRINITY GESE GRADE 10 INTERACTIVE PHASE
TRINITY GESE GRADE 12 LISTENING PHASE
TRINITY GESE GRADE 12 INTERACTIVE PHASE

If you are interested in finding out more information about the books and the author, contact me at:

pashby64@gmail.com

Printed by Amazon Italia Logistica S.r.l.
Torrazza Piemonte (TO), Italy

52992758R00040